The Blood Drives: One Pint Down

By

Duane Anderson

ISBN: 978-81-8253-840-5

First Edition: 2022
Rs. 200/-

Cyberwit.net
HIG 45 Kaushambi Kunj, Kalindipuram
Allahabad - 211011 (U.P.) India
http://www.cyberwit.net
Tel: +(91) 9415091004
E-mail: info@cyberwit.net

Printed in India at VCORRE.

Dedication

To all the men and women who donate blood products for those in need, and those men and women who collect these lifesaving gifts.

Acknowledgements

Adelaide Literary Magazine	"Detective Skills"; "Business Environment"; "Twelve O'clock High"; "Boris Karloff"; "Ms. Know-It-All"; "Omen"; "Bloody Mary"; "Visitor for the Day"
Blue Moon Literary and Art Review	"The Right Combination"
Cholla Needles	"Welcome to One Strange Place"; "The Flash"; "The Blood Drive Comedian"
Fine Lines	"It's Windy Out There"
Ibis Head Review	"The Blood Donating Cow"
Modern Literature	"Friday the Thirteenth"
Oddball Magazine	"Halloween Blood Drive"
Scarlet Leaf Review	"A New Normal"
The Sea Letter	"Executive for a Day"
The Pangolin Review	"One of the Essentials"
The Thieving Magpie	"Which Arm Do You Prefer to Use? - Round Two"; "The Unappreciated Door"; "Doorman"; "Come on Down"; "Preferential Treatment"
Tipton Poetry Journal	"Battleship"
Torrid Literature Journal	"Visibility: The Hallway Greeter"

Contents

Welcome to the Blood Drive

Thank you for coming in today
and helping out with a most needed lifesaving donation.
Thank you, thank you, thank you.
I am the Donor Ambassador,
the first one to greet you
hoping to make your visit a pleasant one.
We don't want to make you nervous

or make your wait time unbearable.
We want you to enjoy your experience
so you want to come back again.
Come on in,
sign-in on the computer,
read the special material on donating,
then take a seat.

Someone will be along soon
to go over your health history
and draw a pint of your blood,
and afterwards,
relax with a few snacks and drinks
then walk on out knowing your blood will help save lives.
Again, we thank you.

Welcome to One Strange Place

"Welcome to Walmart,
how can I help you?",
except we were not at Walmart,
we were at a blood drive,
but that was one of the staff yelled out
to the next donor that walked into the room.

It was just one of those days,
one of those strange days
when anything could happen,
and if that wasn't enough,
two people walked into the lobby
one in a princess costume,
the other one dressed as a T-Rex.

The princess spoke to the receptionist
asking her to call her husband.
When he came out,
I thought he might slay the dragon,
my new name for the T-Rex,
and rescue the princess,
but he did not carry any sword,
so my day dream did not become real.
It must have been a friendly dragon as
the three of them walked out the door,
maybe to eat lunch.

All I know is that
they did not come to the table where I sat,

to sign in and donate their blood.
I'm not even sure if they would have
taken any of the dragon's blood anyway.
I'm pretty sure there isn't much of a demand
for dragon's blood
since one doesn't see a lot of dragons
walking around in this day and age.
Today just happened to be one of those days
when one wandered in.

Lost in a Maze

Walking down the steps
to the lower-level conference room
where the blood drive had been
held the past several years,
other than tables and chairs,
the room is empty of people.

Wondering if the blood drive was cancelled,
and no one notified me of the change,
I walked back up the steps
to the guard's desk,
asking him if there was still a blood drive?

He advised, letting me know
that it was in another conference room
in the lower level.
I walk through a maze of hallways before
I finally reach it,
like a rat finding the cheese
in a maze.

The first two donors failed to show.
Maybe they too thought like I had,
thinking it was cancelled.
I made the decision
to put up arrow signs along the hallways,
hoping to lead them to this room,
as long as they understood the meaning
of the arrow signs.

After all
we weren't here to be lonely.
We wanted visitors to keep us company.

First Time

She said it was her first time donating
and she was worried.
One co-worker came along to comfort her
while other co-workers waiting gave her
a hard time about it being her first time
like some co-workers are known to do.
I make no comment, but if I worked with her,
I know I would have done so too.

They did an excellent job of psyching her up
because during her health history
she was deferred,
her blood pressure being too high.

I think back to when I made my first donation,
but I have no memories of it
whether if I was worried about it or not,
but I passed all the tests
and made my first donation.
I now say there is nothing to worry about
having done it over a hundred times now,
but what do I know?

There may be a next time for her.
What will happen next time,
stay tuned?

Pain Free

He asked if she would believe him
that they had pain free needles today.
It was the special of the day,
for a limited time,
one day only.
She didn't seem to have any faith
in his words.
Maybe she didn't believe in a divine being,
or in miracles.

I experienced the pain free needles last week,
though no one mentioned to me that they
had anything like that in their arsenal.
I didn't feel the needle going into my arm
when I donated blood the week before.
It was pain free for the first time,
and I still don't know how she did it,
but it was great and truly amazing.

At today's blood drive,
did the current donor know the difference
between truth and fiction?
Am I about to witness another miracle?
Maybe he will become a saint,
though he might need a miracle
or two more in addition to this one,
but he has my vote if he pulls this off.

Pin Cushion

He walked through the door
stating that the pin cushion was here.
He should get his wish
as they prick his middle finger
to test his iron count
and later on
place a needle in his arm
to draw a pint of his blood.
Yes, I would say, he will get his wish.

The Greeter

I sit at a table
in the middle of a long hallway
half way between the rear doors of the building
and the cafeteria on the other end.
The foot traffic is heavy at times,
people going in and out of the building,
others going from one room to another,
room to cafeteria,
room to kitchenette,
building to building.

I could try singing
"Oh, What a Beautiful Mornin"
from the musical Oklahoma,
but my singing talent never quite developed.
My dad would ask me to sing Far, Far, Away
whenever I sang.
He knew all about my singing talent,
after all, I had inherited it from him.

I could say welcome to the blood drive
as the people walked by my table,
but most of the people walking by had
no intention of parting with any of their blood,
so instead, I just said good morning
as they pass by over and over again,
trying not to say it more than once
as some passed by multiple times during the day.

At times I felt that I was at the zoo
only that I was one of its residents.
Was I the elephant or monkey
they came to see,
or maybe the baboon or gorilla?
Though no one laughed or screamed out in terror
as they passed by my table,
I took it that my looks might have been average,
and nothing to write home about.

There's no question that
I am definitely along the pathway
to their various destinations,
whether they choose to look at me or not
is up to them,
though I hope they stop to see me.
Right now, it looks like I am the unofficial
hallway greeter for the day.

Have You Ever Donated Under Another Name?

And I think,
no, I have always donated under one name,
the name the parents assigned me,
the name I had no participation in.
It was the name I provided on my donor card,
but then I think some of the other
names that I had been given
over the years,
some by friends, coaches, co-workers.

None of the other names are still used that I know of,
at least I don't hear anyone
calling me one of them any longer,
but still, they are remembered by me,
and maybe they are still worth repeating.

Other names I have been called are probably best forgotten,
and I am sure I have been called other names
that I did not hear
for unknown reasons for something
that someone didn't like what I had done.

No, I never have donated under another name
as this one is as good as it is ever going to get.

Budweiser Blood

I don’t remember their names,
but I will call them Steve and John
who lying on beds, side by side,
start talking to each other.
Steve comments to John
“I see you’re finally donating some of your Budweiser.”
Obviously, his co-worker knows something
that the rest of the world didn’t.

After all, working with someone for years
one tends to learn a few things about a person
and who’s to argue about donating some excess beer.
Do his arteries and veins run on beer rather than blood?
The blood in the bag did look
to have a golden tint to it,
and I’m sure that they will test it
before passing it on to someone in need?
Though, I sure could use a refreshing drink about now,
so go ahead and pour me a cold one
when you get a chance.

Executive for a Day

Free parking was what I was looking for.
I wasn't aware that there were
multiple parking sections.
I only saw the garage open
to a business where I was to work that day,
so I entered,
thinking it was just a garage,
somewhere I could park my car.

Little did I know it at the time,
but I found out as I left to go home
that I had parked in the executive
parking garage,
with only one way in and one way out.

All day I didn't feel like an executive.
I did not sit in an office suite
overlooking the city from the top floor
of the building.
Instead, I sat at a table in a hallway,
no window view,
waiting for clients to show up
for their appointments.

Maybe my car felt important all day long,
though it did not tell me
as we left to go home.

Visibility: The Hallway Greeter

She moved me out of the room
into the hallway after an hour and a half
saying that I wasn't being punished
but my presence in the hallway
would definitely make me more visible
and maybe that would generate more walk-ins.

The hallway was definitely warmer
allowing me to take off my coat
so that I looked as if I was
going to stay rather than ready to leave.
I was glad for the warmer temperature,
and decided the hallway was probably
the best place for me.

After all, I was the donor ambassador,
the first person they would come
in contact with
and the last as they left,
so welcome, welcome, welcome
to the blood drive.
Our beds are open,
just waiting for you.

I was told that I didn't look very excited,
but it is hard to be excited
as people just walk past
leaving me to wait for that next donor.
Maybe I should act more like a carnival barker.

"Come donate your blood,
plenty of free drinks, plenty of free treats.
Come one, come all."
It is a routine I know I will have to work on.

A New Normal

I sat in a hallway of a large food company,
which sitting in a hallway
was nothing unusual for this job.
On the wall across from where I sat,
a television was turned on
showing commercials of some of their products,
from sunflower seeds, pies, jerky,
fajitas, popcorn, frozen dinners,
along with a few recipes using some of their products.
They ran the small selection of their products,
interspersed between a few public relations items,
over and over and over again,
repeating each one every fifteen minutes,
in a continuous loop.
I pretty much had everything all memorized
as I sat there for six straight hours.

Maybe it wasn‘t their intention
for anyone to sit in the hallway
for six hours in front of that screen,
but as it turned out,
it was a form of torture
and I will never be the same.
After that day, my wife had me committed,
and now I wear a strait jacket,
watching Looney Tunes cartoons all day long.
It is my new life, my new normal,
living here with the others in my new home.

A Very Slow Day

The donors trickled in,
at a rate of about two an hour.
I knew even molasses traveled at a faster pace than this.
Maybe very few showed up at work today
which I tended to doubt was true being weeks away
from a holiday and the driving conditions were good.

For some reason there seemed to have been little promotion
to get anyone to sign up for the blood drive.
Maybe word didn't get out that we would be here.
It is early December,
Christmas songs are playing on the radio,
most of them sung by Bing Crosby.

What a better gift than to give a pint of their blood,
the holiday spirit,
the blood which could save the lives of up to three people.
I say be a Santa rather than a Scrooge,
but it just wasn't meant to be today,
because unfortunately, the blood drive was a well-kept secret.

I would have donated a pint myself today,
but I had another month to go before
I was eligible again,
so that option was out.
Maybe my time would be better spent
by walking around with a sign

stating that walk-ins were needed.
Due to a lack of donors showing up,
I had plenty of time to enjoy the scenery as
I looked out at the Missouri River
from the window from where I sat.
Two trees stood next to the river

full of robins yet to have flown south for the winter.
The trees, still full of berries for them to feast on
since the ground was too hard for them
to get their usual meal of earth worms.
Maybe when their food source disappeared
they would head south for the winter.

In the meantime, between my glances outside,
I wait for that next donor
as I listen to another Christmas song
sung by Bing Crosby.

Pour a Little Out So You Don't Wear It

As he laid on the donation bed,
she asked him if he wanted anything to drink,
being an accommodating host,
like a bottle of water or
can of cranberry or orange juice,
the only three drinks that are stocked at the blood drive.
He said he would take a bottle of water,
so she cracked open the water bottle
and said "I'll pour a little out
so you don't wear it"
since the bottle was very full
and accidents like spilling a little water on one's clothes
have been known to happen.

She was being helpful since he only had one arm
available as blood was being drawn from the other.
It is hard finding many people
wanting to get their clothes wet
no matter where that may be,
and no one was holding a wet T-shirt contest today
so I guess there really was no reason for anybody getting wet.
No one wants to stay wet and uncomfortable
until their clothes get a chance to dry out,
unless you are one of the strange ones
that always carries an extra spare set of clothes to change into.

It was a blood drive,
and of course, no one wanted to wear
any blood on their clothes either,

but then again, that did not happen.
Blood wasn't something that was poured
out of the collection bags
once they had finished with their donation.
It was collected to save lives, not spilled.

Everything went as planned,
as expected,
as hoped,
with another dry donor experience.

Raised Hands

The first three donors all finished
up at the same time
even though they began at different times.
Each of them holding one arm up in the air
with the other hand placing pressure on
the spot where the needle had just been pulled from.

It was if they were asking to be called upon
by a teacher for a question they knew the answer to
or had a question for someone else in the room,
or maybe they were just volunteering
to donate another pint on the next blood drive held there.

Maybe their hands were raised because
they all had to use the restroom,
but they weren't waving them frantically back and forth
like they could no longer hold it in
and weren't ready to pee in their pants,
so I ruled that option out,
and I too raised my arm just to be ornery,
but like the others,
none of us were called upon.

As the others lowered their arms,
the phlebotomists' bandaged their arms
to stop the blood from flowing out,
and I too put my arm down
so I no longer looked like a fool,
more than I already did,

after all, I was just the donor ambassador
volunteering my services for the day.
My day for donating whole blood
would come on another day.

Mind Reader

He did his mind reading routine
with the next donor waiting.
"You must be Jane Doe" he said
as he picked up the name tag
setting on the table.
There was no one else waiting at the time,
so it wasn't much of an effort
for him to make his deduction.
I like to think that even I could have done that,
but I am reminded myself
that he is the mind reader, not me.
Maybe he would read her mind once again
and say "I bet you are here to donate blood?",
and she would say, "My, aren't you amazing,
reading my mind twice now."

Would he next become a fortune teller
and also tell her of her fortune?
I wasn't close enough to hear what went on next,
but I didn't see him carrying a crystal ball either.
Maybe he would hand her a fortune cookie instead?
There is always more than one way
to discover one's fortune, that,
and holding a winning lottery ticket sure doesn't hurt.
It is a fortune I myself wouldn't mind holding,
but the fortune today wasn't a lottery ticket or fortune cookie.
Instead, it was the life-giving gift of blood
that each person would donate.

I Would If I Could

People passing by are curious as to why
I am sitting at a table with stickers
and sheets of paper covering the table.
After all, not every day was there
a blood drive here, with me
sitting in the middle of a lobby
waiting for donors to show up.

One observer read the sign at the table
and said that he had given enough blood.
I was at a Veterans Administration Hospital
and I am sure that he had given more than
enough blood for his country already.
He kept on walking after making his comment,
and I did not bother asking him anything further.

There were others who wished to donate
but could not because they served overseas
during a certain time period and were deferred,
and others were unable because they were
on multiple medications,
or in wheel chairs and would be unable
to get onto the bus where the blood was being drawn.

They were the ones, who stated,
I would if I could
and I fully understood what they were saying.
It is mostly the medical staff who had
made appointments to donate their blood that day.
This was their way of serving
for those others who could not.

Precious Life Saving Treasures

I was surrounded by display cases
filled with diamond rings, necklaces, watches,
and other items of precious jewels and metals
with names like Cartier, Mont Blanc,
and other names too foreign to me
since jewelry was not something that
I was very familiar with.

I was more familiar with names
like Cheap-Skate and Bargain Brands,
items more in my price range,
but all of it held no special interest for me
since I was here for a blood drive.
It was only a building where
I would spend some time at,
a location to check people in
before they made their donation.

Security cameras and an army of guards were
in place to protect all the jewelry,
and the blood, it was temporarily stored in boxes
protected with ice to keep it safe
for the time being until it was
taken to a storage site
waiting for a final shipment to a hospital.

The blood donated today to be used
to save lives later on was a more precious
treasure than all the diamonds,
gold, and silver inside this building.

Support Your Local Jeweler

A local jewelry store was hosting a blood drive today.
The store covered half a football field at least,
but I was only eyeballing the size of the room,
and not scoping it out for any jewelry heist.

I was here to welcome the blood donors
as they came into the building,
but to also let them know
that they could do some shopping

if they wished while they were waiting,
and that I would let them know when
the next opening was available.
I wasn't James Gardner,

though I was reminded of his movie
Support Your Local Sheriff as I said it,
though I wasn't there to
support a local jewelry store.

Maybe not everything in the store was out of their
price range and it may not be an everyday need
like groceries or personal care items,
but like most things, jewelry was a necessity for some,

though everyone didn't come here to shop
for rings, necklaces, earrings or watches.
Instead, some came here to donate their blood,
and shopping for jewelry was secondary

or maybe just a curiosity,
but I wasn't going to stop them
from supporting their local jewelry store
if that was to their choosing.

The Blood Donating Cow

Sometimes I feel like a dairy cow when
lying on the bed donating blood,
but rather than placing a milking machine
on udders which I am pretty sure I am void of,
a needle is placed in my arm,
and instead of streams of white milk flowing,
red blood flows out of my vein into
the waiting arms of a collection bag.

Both fluids serve a purpose, one used as a drink
or maybe poured on your morning Fruit Loops
or made into some other food product,
and the other used whole or separated into
its parts of platelets, plasma, and red blood cells
to be transfused to another later on.
I am the faithful cow showing up
at my designated time frame

ready to get milked once again,
though I find that the quantity of the fluids
from cows and I is quite different.
The cows win that contest hands down,
or should I say, udders down,
and also winning how often they are milked,
twice a day to my once every other month routine.
As for saving lives from the use of my donation,

I think I definitely win that contest
as it is given to another in need.

Now if I was at a sperm bank,
things would be quite different.
I would be more than willing in making
multiple deposits several times a day.
I guess the frequency on giving all depends
on the type of fluids being donated.

Feast or Famine

Everything was going just great,
the donors were arriving on time
and they were able to donate,
then a famine reared its ugly head,
and it wasn't because they were no longer
showing up for their appointments

nor that the rains didn't come
and the sun scorched the earth.
No, after nine successful donations
the next four appointments were deferred
from giving for various reasons,
knowing full well that a few deferrals

were expected during a blood drive.
I made a comment in jest
stating that their standards were set too high
but knowing full well that having
a safe blood supply was essential,
and finally, another came in and broke

the string of deferrals,
then blood flowed once again.
Yes, let the rivers of blood from
the veins continue to flow,
a feast from the gods
soon to be given to those in need.

Traffic Flow

The company probably didn’t have a traffic
division in charge of room and hallway gridlock
like a city’s public works department
in charge of stop sign and traffic light placements.
Maybe they had a safety director to handle

all the traffic flows within the building,
but a special three-way mirror could have been used
as donors exited the room being used for
the blood drive into a busy corridor so they could have
easily seen the traffic coming from both directions,

or maybe just a stop sign was required,
or at least a yield sign to make sure that
they stopped or at a minimum slowed down
at the doorway, looking both left and right
before exiting the room.

After all, we didn’t want any injuries
requiring medical attention since they were
already wearing a bandage where
the needle had been removed from their arm.
I am assuming the ones in the corridor

had the right-of-way, but there was
a blind spot for those leaving the room.
The sign didn’t need to be permanent
and could be placed by the doorway just for the day.
Luckily, there had been no collisions,

though there were a few close calls
requiring a little dancing of the jig
to avoid crashing into the passing traffic,
and I guess their safety record was maintained
for another day, thirty-three donors and no injuries

I Make a Difference

They handed me a sticker
after I signed in at the blood bank
with the 'I Make a Difference' slogan.
Maybe I did make a difference
donating my blood, something that
not enough people seem to volunteer in giving.
Sometimes it may be the fear of a needle,
not knowing what to expect,
and others not caring at all,

too busy for something like this.
I wasn't told that I made a difference
when I ordered the cheeseburger for lunch,
or when I went to the supermarket
to pick up a few grocery items,
or filled my gas tank at the filling station.
I might have been thanked for coming
to these places and purchasing their products,
but I sure wasn't told I made a difference.

I know my blood won't get used today,
but after it is tested, I know
it will be passed on to some hospital
to be given to a patient in need,
and then I will know for sure
that I truly made a difference,
and I guess that is why I and others
continue donating our blood year after year,
knowing that we are doing some good in the world.

Friday the Thirteenth

The sign-up sheet lying on the table said
the next blood drive for this location would be
held on July 13th which meant it would be
on a Friday the Thirteenth.
It is occasionally bound to happen

since they always scheduled
this event on a Friday, and knowing that there
might be a few superstitious people
in this strange world of ours who may not
sign up because of this fear,

maybe it is best that they stay home
in bed and sleep the day away, having
remembering once seeing someone who didn't
want to sign his name on the thirteenth line
on the sign-in sheet so he skipped that line

and signed his name on the fourteenth line
which still made his name the thirteenth on the sheet,
something he couldn't get around unless
the next person that came filled their name
on the blank line above his.

I know of no time when it isn't a good time
to donate, even if it is on Friday the Thirteenth.
Well, maybe there are a few exceptions,
like in the time of some disaster,
in the middle of a fire, tornado, or hurricane.

The blood being donated will be accepted on
each and every day, even if it is given on Friday
the Thirteenth, so not to worry, your gift
of blood will be more than welcomed,
but bring your good luck charm with you just in case.

Which Arm Do You Prefer to Use?

At the blood drive
they usually ask people which
arm they prefer to use
since the vein in one arm

may be better than the other,
but in this case,
having only one arm,
there really was no need to ask,

and if they did ask just out of habit,
she could always tell them to
take a wild guess and one would think
it shouldn't take them very long

to make that determination.
After all, it wasn't like they were some
barker at the carnival trying to guess
her weight or age to win a prize.

Tinted World

Looking out the windows it looked cloudy outside,
so I was glad to be inside working at the blood drive
since I couldn't get a lot done outside anyway if it was going to rain,
only to find out that the windows were all tinted,

and my thinking changed somewhat.
It felt good volunteering my services at the drive,
but I sure would have felt
a whole lot better if someone hadn't

told me that the windows were tinted,
and it was gorgeous outside.
Sometimes, we live in a tinted world,
and things are not what they seem.

When I look into the mirror
to see how I look,
sometimes I see beauty,
other times I wish I hadn't looked.

It's Windy Out There

As people walked into the building,
most told the guard at the front desk
that it was really windy out there,

or it's a little windy out there,
or just it's windy out there,
as they struggled opening the door

from the suction caused by the strong winds.
He already knew that it was windy from looking
outside and seeing the flag waving,

the tree branches moving back and forth,
the leaves from last fall blowing
across the parking lot, and

light poles swaying back and forth.
The guard told me that he couldn't
wait for three o'clock to get here

so he didn't have to hear those words
from anyone one more time.
I just laughed knowing I only

had to be here two hours less than he.
They may have been talking to the guard,
but sitting at a table close to where he was sitting,

I couldn't help but hear all the same comments,
though someone had directed one comment to me of
at least you're not getting blown away in here.

I guess I should have brought a kite along
to fly if there was a slow period during the day,
but it was probably too windy even for that.

Before I left at the end of my shift, I couldn't
help myself and told the guard that I guess
it was time for me to head home

and hope the winds didn't blow me away.
I was sure he would appreciate
hearing those words one more time.

Warm Thoughts Don't Always Comfort

She came into the room seeming well prepared.
Maybe she didn't come with a back pack
filled with food and water, camping gear,
and a Swiss army pocket knife, but brought
along a blanket to keep her warm
as she laid on the bed while donating blood
knowing very well that the room would be
kept cooler than the rest of the building
based on her past experiences.

I was sorry I didn't have any hot chocolate
to give her to warm her up some as she finished,
and for that matter, sorry there wasn't
any for me either, or a fire going in the fireplace,
though there was no fireplace in the first place.
The best I could do was offering her
warm thoughts, thanking for her for
coming in today as she raced out of the room
hoping to warm herself up in any way she could.

Seven Plus

He marked his blood type as seven plus.
It wasn't a blood type that I had ever seen before,
since all the blood types always began with

a letter followed by a plus or minus sign.
It could have been a secret code
that required a special decoder ring

or decipher sheet in order to break the code,
or it could have been that he had already given
seven plus gallons since he started donating years ago,

then again, it could have been because it was
seven o'clock in the morning and he
had already marked seven as his arrival

time and appointment time and
hadn't fully awaken yet from it still being
very early in the morning and continued on

writing sevens into the next column.
The brain powers had yet to reach full power,
though he did remember his name and

that his appointment time was at seven and
maybe that his blood type was at least positive.
It wasn't perfect, but it was a pretty good start of the day.

Halloween Blood Drive

Halloween came,
and where am I,
but at a blood drive.
Six or seven donors came dressed in costume
and I missed my opportunity.
I could have dressed as Count Dracula,
and could have said as each one showed up,
“We want your blood, please sign this sheet.”

Which Arm Do You Prefer to Use? – Round Two

When donors come into give blood, they
get asked which arm they prefer to use.
Did they prefer to use their dominate arm, all

depending if they were right or left-handed,
or one that matched their political leanings,
whether they were liberal or conservative,

or that they just chose to alternate arms each time
they donated to give each arm an equal opportunity
of getting used? Some don't have a preference

and take whatever bed is currently open,
while others have a vein in one arm that is
more prominent than the other.

Today's totals were eleven for the left arm
and nine for the right, though one of those donors
choosing the right arm found out that they

were not successful in drawing any of his blood
from that arm, the well came up dry after they tried
multiple times repositioning the needle to find

that magical vein, so being the gracious donor that
he was, and still wishing to donate, he let them
try the other arm, and the second time they struck

gold on the first attempt, for if it too had turned out to be unsuccessful, he would have run out of arms for them to try with.

Now he had two bandaged arms and could tell everyone that he had given twice to shame those choosing not to sign up.

The Unappreciated Door

Most came into the building
using the door on the right side,
but when they exited the building,
they still used the exact same door, though now
it was considered a door on the left side.

Both doors were unlocked and
I did not hear one of the doors, saying "Use me,
use me," though maybe I wasn't listening.
I didn't understand their use of the same
door coming and going into the building,

especially when it wasn't always the closest
door to them. I was one of those people who
always chose the door on the right side and
not because I was right-handed,
but I had the habit of staying in the right

hand lanes when driving and continued the
habit of staying on the right side when
walking on a sidewalk or using a door.
I could see one using the same door when
activating the switch on the automatic door

if they were handicapped since the
device only worked on the one door,
and I also figured out it didn't have anything
to do with being right brained or left brained
since I was considered left brained

and still continued to use the door on the right side,
but I knew it still had something to do with the brain,
but it wasn't a no brainer to me, it was something
that I would never figure out as I sat there
watching people coming and going for five hours.

The Flash

I was in a medical building, but at
least it wasn't me in a hospital where
I was the one needing medical attention.

For that, I was extremely happy, and ready
to celebrate, knowing that I have had more
than my share of visits in one in recent years.

Instead, the building I was in was a medical
school student center, waiting for students, doctors,
nurses, or anyone else willing to donate.

Some of the students had class schedules
that they wanted to maintain, and needed
to get finished in a certain time frame

in order to not be late for their classes,
but I could not arrange any guarantees,
for I wasn't the one drawing their blood.

I was only there to check them in, having no
special powers to control the amount of time it took,
though at times, one could get through fairly quickly,

but no one could expect them to move as fast as
The Flash. Yes, the phlebotomists were super heroes,
but they didn't quite move at super hero speeds.

Perfect Attendance

I had no idea how often it happened at the
various blood drives taking place across
the country each day, but it was bound to
happen at some point, or I really hoped I

would see it happen sometime, and that milestone
event was for perfect attendance, where everyone
making an appointment to give blood,
actually showing up, knowing it was totally beyond

anyone's control getting everyone to show up,
but still, it was good to see it finally happening.
Even though it took a lot longer than I ever imagined,
I hoped the next time I witnessed this, that it would

take place much quicker. To celebrate the occasion,
I toasted with a can of cranberry juice along with
a package of chocolate chip cookies left over from
the snack canteen table, and rang the bell, a leftover

from the past, still stored in the registration tote, the bell, a piece
of history, once used to congratulate donors when they had
reached another gallon mark, and now, to let those still
remaining in the room know that something special just hap-
pened.

Detective Skills

I was about to ask her if she was donating today
since she had done so previously at the
past two blood drives, but then I remembered
that she gave double reds the last time and

wasn't cligible to give again until the next drive.
After working at the same location many times over the
past few years, one tended to remember certain things and
recognize a few of the regulars, either by the names on

the scheduled donor list or by their faces as
they walked by the table where I sat. I recognized
her face, but then again, I had a second clue,
there probably weren't a lot of people

working at this company with only one arm,
so my Sherlock Holmes' skills were finally
kicking in. Watch out Dr. Watson, I may be
taking over your Sherlock sidekick job sometime soon.

Business Environment

The business environment had changed since I
was last in the working world. The dress code seemed
to be a thing of the past, though some kinds of
clothes were still required, but shorts, T-shirts, and

flip flops seemed to be the favorite business attire of the day.
Then in the designated multi-purpose room,
ping pong tables, pool tables, foosball tables,
bean bag toss, and video games, PCs, free soft drinks,

and even a bar with four kinds of beer on tap were all in
wait for anyone's use, and indulge they did, but they weren't
hanging around this room all the time, so I assumed
work was still performed during certain times of the day.

Once, even I was glad when the company I
worked for did away with the suit and tie dress code,
and went to corporate casual, but as to wearing
shorts and T-shirts to work, I just wouldn't feel right,

being old fashioned in some respects, so it was
good that I left the working world when I did,
knowing I wouldn't have fit in this new dynamic universe,
still preferring to wear a dress shirt, pants,

and casual shoes as I volunteered at companies
like this, and as for the games, I too had no use
for them, preferring work over playing games.
Yes, I am different, a dinosaur of the past.

Twelve O'clock High

Someone had signed up to donate at noon,
but I could not tell from the list of scheduled
donors if that person was female or male based
on the name they had provided on the schedule,

not that it mattered. It was more of my own
curiosity than anything else, having
only provided a first name of G and
a last name of K on the appointment sheet.

I found both names were short, and easy
to pronounce, but now, I must wait to
see if they show up to find out if G K
was their real name, a nickname,

or maybe just the first initials of their name?
Show time, showdown, begins at twelve
o'clock noon, but there isn't going to be any
shootout like at the OK Corral, or any contest

to see who can bleed the fastest. Instead,
there will be an unveiling of who our mystery
person of the day is, but if you are the Agatha
Christie type, maybe you can solve it ahead of time.

Boris Karloff

His last name was Karloff,
so I just had to ask,
I couldn't help myself,

if he was any relation to Boris,
but there was no Boris connection,
it wasn't meant to be today

as I travelled down memory lane
of watching horror films of old, and then
I looked again at the list of scheduled donors,

but there wasn't anyone on it with the last name of
Price, so there was no need to ask anyone if they had
a father or grandfather with the first name of Vincent,

but there was someone with the last name of Luther,
but I wasn't going to ask them either about a first name
of Lex, since he was a comic book villain, and I was

still on the horror film theme which had completely
taken control of my thought process, and was also a
reminder that it was only days away from Halloween.

Questions

She asked if I had any questions with any
of the health history questions, but I had an
issue with the number of questions asked.
There were too many.
They were all yes and no questions,
but I was looking for a third option,
that of none of the above
because I didn't know any of the answers,
including the question
if I was feeling well today.
I was failing and
that was my life, not knowing.
My real problem was with the answers,
looking for answers of which I had none.
I had only questions,
none of which would be answered today.

Doorman

I did not know why they had me sitting
in the lobby where I sat all alone,
with only the television to keep me company,

something I wished would have been turned off
as the station they had it turned to had
programs on it that I found boring as hell,

though there must have been a few
others that found the shows entertaining
for them to still be on the air.

The front door of the company was locked,
with no intercom anywhere in site to
accommodate visitors to speak with someone within

the building in order to let them in, but I soon
found out that I had another job to perform,
that of being the unofficial doorman for the day,

so from time to time I looked outside to see if
anyone stood in front of the door waiting,
even though I wasn't a security guard,

having no uniform, or badge, or radio to
communicate with any other security personnel,
to let the visitors into the building.

My Name Now Is Denise, But Once Was David

The first question on the health history
questionnaire asked if I was male or female,
but I considered myself as a
homosexual transgender female transvestite,
born as a male,
but now considered myself as
being a transgender female
who liked dating other females,
but also liked wearing men's clothing,
so there I was,
trying to figure out what to
mark on the questionnaire,
once again confused by the
only two options allowed.

Poster Boy

Some came into the room wearing hand guns
and handcuffs, though the guns were holstered
and the handcuffs weren't attached onto anyone's wrists.
Instead, they hung from belts and shoulder straps,
and seeing things like this weren't unexpected since
the blood drive was held at a police station.
Their hardware was just part of their daily
wardrobe as they performed their jobs on the streets.
There were no shoot-outs or arrests made during my
visit there, and I was on my best behavior, that of a
choir boy, with a halo hanging high above my head.
I was a saint rather than being my usual self,
knowing it was never good to be posted on anyone's
ten most wanted list, especially at a facility like this.

Strange Day

It was one of those days when unusual
things took control beginning
when a young man came to the front door in,
thinking that he had come to make a blood donation,
only to find out he was lost, having recently
moved to thc city and not familiar with his
way around town. He said he had already received
directions to where he lived after talking to a police officer,
but for whatever reason was unable to follow them,
and wandered around for two hours in the
rain before showing up at our door,
then off he went after giving him a new set of directions,
to continue his adventures in this mystical city,
hoping this time his search of finding
his home would end in success.

And a little while later, a young woman came wandering
in after first tethering two dogs she had been walking
to a bench in front of the building stating she had
locked herself out of her apartment and asked
if she could use the phone to make a call,
and after several attempts
with no one answering her calls,
she left, untying her dogs from the bench
and continued on, walking to places unknown.

I kept waiting for someone else to appear
with another situation not usually
encountered on a blood drive,

maybe The Lone Ranger riding a horse in need of
a pooper scooper to pick up what the horse left behind,
or a clown riding a unicycle, asking if we had an air pump
to repair a flat tire, but after those first two,
the only ones to come through the door
were the donors with an appointment,
and I was okay knowing things were back to normal,
for nothing was wrong with normal,
but the abnormal surely broke up the day.

Christmas Portrait

After each donating a unit of blood
the week before Christmas,
a husband and wife
pose for a picture,
each holding the bags they had
filled just minutes before
as they smile into the camera,
maybe to be used
as their holiday picture and
mailed to their children,
their friends, and relatives
showing others that it was
better to give than receive.
They were Santa's helpers today,
giving the gift of life to others,
to those in need of its saving powers.

Battleship

She said she was playing battleship,
a game of hits and misses,
and it was all hits for her today,
not sinking any battleships

with all of her hits,
but sticking the needle in the vein
and each time drawing blood on the
first try. A perfect record,

nothing less but what was expected
to each laying down on the beds
as they donated a unit of their blood.
It was smooth sailing in calm waters.

Are You Here to Donate?

Sitting in a high traffic hallway
where hundreds passed by,
I thought about asking each person
as they walked by my table
if they were here to donate,
but I kept quiet as they passed.
It wasn't like I was trying to save my voice
to sing at a concert later that evening,
or give a lecture at some university,
but I refrained, not wanting to
have to listen to my voice
since I didn't possess one of those
Walter Cronkite news anchor voices,
one that one enjoyed listening to,
or to a long-playing record that
kept skipping over and over again,
and repeating:
"Are you here to donate?"
"Are you here to donate?"
"Are you here to donate?"

Bloodletting

She arrived a few minutes early for her appointment,
asking if there were any other openings for the
bloodletting so she could text her husband
with the open time slots. I wondered if she was
really one of those who still believed that all illnesses

stemmed from an overabundance of blood and it
was the reason why she decided on donating today,
or was she offering her blood as a sacrifice to the gods,
or that it allowed her to enter a trance-like state
to experience visions of celestial beings or of lost

ancestors, or maybe it was a smorgasbord of all of the above?
The methods of drawing blood had improved since those
early days of bloodletting from once opening a vein with
a sharp piece of wood, or if one was lucky, leeches
may have performed this bloodshed centuries ago,

where now a needle, a hose, and a bag
were used in the collection process. Maybe that
is how I unknowingly kept healthier all these years,
ridding myself of my own overabundance of blood,
and not needing to take any of those medicines

that were constantly advertised on television
with those strange sounding names as if they
were part of some science fiction novel,
Cialis, Trulicity, Zantac, Lyrica, Xeljanz, Vraylar,
correcting everything from erectile dysfunction to

treating manic or mixed episodes of bipolar disorder in adults.
In the end, her husband must have decided against making
an appointment, guessing the tradition of bloodletting
wasn't his thing, and favored keeping all of his blood
in its current location, where most were willing to give

someone their overabundance to another in need.
It might not have been any cure to the one on the giving end,
but was a lifer saver to the one on the other end,
and whatever you wanted to call the process,
the end result was definitely satisfying and worthwhile.

Aliases

Six hours of being cooped up in a room
located in the local police station,
I sometimes felt I was in a prison cell,
only without the bars and prison attire,

and there wasn't any need in using my one phone
call to talk to a lawyer or a bail bondsman
to post any bail for I was carrying my get-
out-of-jail-free Monopoly card in my wallet.

I also noticed my mug shot wasn't included
in any of the pictures posted on their
bulletin board, so I guess I was no longer
wanted for being too ugly, though

I was asked if I had ever donated under
any prior names and told them that I had;
Bugsy Siegal, Al Capone, Baby Face Nelson,
Clyde Barrow among a few others,

but hadn't used any of them in recent days.
Finally, after completing my short sentence,
volunteering for a six-hour shift of my local civic duty,
I was released under my own recognizance.

Ms. Know-It-All

She seemed to consider herself an expert
after only donating one time prior,
and from the look that she gave me,
I definitely got the warning signal that it was

beneath her needing to review the advance
reading material on this visit to determine
if any important updates had been added.
Maybe it wasn't like the weather changing

hour by hour, or even day to day,
but some people have learned that not all things
in the world remained constant and liked to
keep informed, but unfortunately, not all were

as lucky as her, the expert Ms. Know-It-All
bursting with all of this superior intelligence and
keeping it all to herself, and even if she did want to
share a little bit of this knowledge, I knew I wouldn't

have enough time in the day to listen to all of this
great wisdom, though maybe I should have
been honored just to be in her presence, or at
least that is what I sensed from our brief encounter.

Omen

After years of always holding the blood drive
on a Friday, the day of the week was changed
to a Thursday hoping to get a few additional
employees to volunteer in donating since many of
them were now allowed to work from home on Fridays.
Yes, in theory, the change made sense, but it must
have also jinx the blood drive for a winter blizzard
to occur on the very first day of the change,
with a large percentage of the scheduled donors
failing to show up for their appointment.
I was use to observing them as they came through
the doors from outside from working on past drives
at this location, but few walked into the building today.
Blame it on the change of the day,
blame it on the weather,
an omen, maybe telling them that
some changes just weren't meant to be.

Bloody Mary

As I laid on one of the beds in the
process of donating a pint of blood,
with a needle stuck in one arm,
she asked me if I wanted a juice or a cocktail
instead of asking if I wanted
some juice or a bottle of water.
I said yes, I would take a Bloody Mary,

but she rescinded her offer on the cocktail
after realizing her mistake, and I ended
taking her up on a can of cranberry juice,
the closest thing resembling the color of the
Bloody Mary that I had earlier requested,
trying to make the best of the situation
from my latest disappointment in life.

Visitor for the Day

I signed in at the front desk,
first typing in my name into the computer,
then took two steps back

as it snapped a picture of my face that
would be printed on the visitor badge I
was advised I was required to wear at

all times while I was in the building.
Besides asking my name,
the computer only asked who I was seeing,

but it did not ask the reason for my visit,
and I guess I should have felt fortunate
a brain scan wasn't required to siphon any

remaining memories that were stored in my head,
or swabbing my cheek to obtain my DNA,
or taking my fingerprints for further verification.

I was just visiting there for the day, but felt my presence
was made more important than it should have been
by requiring my name and taking my picture.

I would have been happy just to have
remained as being someone unknown,
a status that would return as I left for the day.

Bullseye

The phlebotomist salivated as he showed
both of his arms to her,
the large veins sticking out from each arm,
like a roadkill to a vulture
or a wounded gazelle to a leopard,
just waiting for a needle to enter
to draw some blood from it,
saying, 'Hey look at us, aren't we something!'
It was an easy target,
as easy as they come.
Bullseye.

Sleight of Hand

After showing me her photo ID,
and handed it back to her after recording
her name from it for my records,
she placed it back into her pocket.
Only a few seconds had gone by when
she asked if I was going to return her
driver's license back to her.
I asked her to look into her back pocket,
and she was amazed at finding it there.

My magical skills, my sleight of hand,
had been truly dazzling and sensational,
though it didn't hurt that she had had
a temporary lapse of memory.
Later in the day, I will see what other
feats of magic that I could attempt next,
maybe pulling a rabbit out of my hat,
or cutting someone in half, but for now,
I was happy with my one feat of magic.

Feast or Famine – Round II

The feast began when donor after donor
showed up for their appointments,
keeping everyone busy drawing their blood

at the blood drive, and now, the feast had ended,
quick as a lightning strike, the famine began when
no one had scheduled any appointments for the next

few hours for time-slots no one seemed to care about.
Maybe now was the time to bring in
the pied piper to play his pipe,

hoping to get a few followers to join him
so he could lead them to into the donation
room to end the famine,

telling them true stories on the lives
that had been saved from past donations,
and that their own donation could do the same,

and if the heartwarming stories didn't work,
they could always try to incent them with
the offer of free snacks and drinks that were available.

Be Positive

He signed in at the front table,
telling his co-worker directly behind him
that he had a blood type of A negative,
while his co-worker quickly pulled the donor
card out of his wallet and showed it to him,
proudly saying he needed to be positive
which also happened to be his blood type,
and seemed very pleased with his words of wisdom.
All of the blood types were welcomed,
whether they were any combination of A, B, or O,
or if it were negative or positive.
It just happened that his blood type
had such a positive message to it,
be positive rather than be negative,
and was very honored to be blessed with it.
Yes, be positive, be happy.
Give, and someone will always welcome your gift.

You've Been Phlebotomized

Phlebotomists drew blood for a living.
They were not Draculas' telling donors
that they wanted to drink their blood.
Yes, they wanted your blood, that was their job,
but only to be used to help save the lives of others,
so what does one say when they are through
taking someone's blood?
You've been phlebotomized,
which sort of sounded like being lobotomized,
making it sound worse than it really was,
or did the term make it more exciting
as one told others about what just happened to them?
The phlebotomists joked around about using the word
at one of their blood drives, not knowing it was
a real word and thinking one day it would be added
to the dictionary as words are added each year.
Yes, you have just been phlebotomized,
whether it was just a trickle, an ooze, a drain,
a seep, a gush, or a spurt, you bled for a good cause.

Preferential Treatment

She used one of those pain free needles
when she drew my blood at the blood bank,
the same kind that she used
the last time when drawing my blood,
one where you didn't feel the stick going in.
I asked her where they purchased these needles,
not that I was going to buy any for myself
since I had no desire to draw my own blood,
or from anyone else for that matter.
Did she get them out just for those special donors,
like me, considering myself to be one of the special ones?
It made her smile knowing that she
did a fine job at sticking me with the needle,
being a pro that she was,
and it probably didn't hurt that I had
large veins, and had gone through
this process many, many times over the years.
Yes, pain free needles, you have to love them.

Come on Down

She wanted to say 'Come on Down'
as what was said on one of the game shows,
but this wasn't The Price Is Right.
They did ask you your name,
plus, a host of other questions,

and upon answering the questions correctly,
you passed the test for donating your blood,
and when finished, you might not win any money,
a car, or a trip to some resort island, but instead,
offered some fruit juice, water, plus a few other snacks.

She was the next one in line,
the next contestant at the blood drive,
where everyone was a finalist, each one a winner
as they donated a unit of their blood,
super heroes, saving lives.

There was no aisle to for anyone to walk on down,
so ignoring the temptation of saying 'Come on Down',
she just said 'Come on Over'.
It just didn't have the same effect,
but she had time to work on her own catchphrase.

Pointed Toward Heaven

As I got onto the elevator to go up,
the sign for the blood drive pointed straight up.
There were only three floors to the building.
Was it being held on the second floor,
the third floor, the roof, or maybe even toward heaven?
Heaven would have been appropriate
for all the good that was going to take place.

I wasn't sure how to get to heaven myself,
but some day, I too may find my way there.
I ended up going to the third floor,
the highest floor this elevator would take me,
and found my way to the event,
even though the arrow sign still pointed
up toward the heavens.

The Right Combination

I attempted holding everyone hostage,
saying no one could pass by me in the hallway
unless they signed up for the blood drive,

but being armed with only a rubber band,
no one took me seriously and walked on by.
It was worth a try, attempting

to fill in all the remaining vacancies
since the WALK-INS welcome sign
did not seem to be working,

for not one person stopped to sign up.
Maybe next time, I would bring along
a flashing neon light sign, repeating

the same message, and me, wearing a clown suit,
seeking to lure them in, working at it,
until I found the right combination.

A Bed Too Tall

She made the mistake of asking if the bed was
higher than usual, or if she was just getting shorter
as she struggled getting onto the bed
in order to donate some blood at the blood drive.
Her fellow employees appropriately replied,

kidding her that she was definitely getting shorter.
She could have practiced getting up on the bed,
vaulting like a pole vaulter
or by taking a running start, leaping up
like a high jumper at a track meet,

but there were no pads of foam
to protect her fall in case of missing her mark,
but in the end, she was given the option
of using a step stool or a step ladder,
satisfying her needs in reaching this goal.

Welcome, Blood Drive Donors

Sitting at a table at the front entrance
of a local Walmart store,
close to their greeter stood as he took
care of customers coming and going,

I too would greet anyone if they came
to my table for assistance, after all,
I was shopping for Walmart's customers,
hoping to get a few walk-ins for the blood drive,

something few and far between
the hundreds that came into shop,
an item not found on their shopping list.
In front of our table, a large sign was displayed,

informing everyone passing by who we were
and the purpose for our visit,
but I wasn't allowed access to the store's intercom
to say, 'Welcome, Blood Drive Donors,

look what specials we have in store for you.'
I just sat there at the table, trying my best
to be one of their poster boys, hoping to slowly
reel in a few of the store's customers to donate.

Meet Super Phlebotomist

She looked to be alive
and in good health
when first entering the room,
not showing any signs
of a walking zombie look,

but the phlebotomist was unable to find
her pulse and asked his co-worker to help,
then had trouble finding her vein
and once again, asked for his help.
The co-worker didn't fly,

have super speeds, or superhuman strength,
but was a man of knowledge,
experience, and dedication.
Meet Super Phlebotomist,
to the rescue, twice in one day.

One of the Essentials

Ads on television, pleas on the evening news,
soliciting people for blood donations,
blood products still needed at hospitals,
one of the essential items,
like the food from grocery stores,
and medicines from pharmacies.

Blood drives at companies,
cancelled. Falling dominoes,
as companies closed down,
not considered essential,
more people working from home,
laid off, no life raft in site.

I do my small part,
making an appointment,
one of the regulars,
part of the blood squad.
Now, more items back on the shelf,
lifesaving essentials.

Customer Care

Some demanded,
Take good care of me,
or I'm never coming back,

while I dreamed of someone receiving
my blood, able to live another day,
another night,

given that second chance.
Yes, everyone was special,
all welcomed into their home,

the red carpet rolled out.
Lay down, close your eyes,
listen to the music playing

as they perform their magic,
and the miracle to be performed later
as the blood is given to another in need.

Empty Beds

Empty beds, lonely,
sitting there
like an abandoned memory,
waiting to be visited,
whether it is from you or me,
they have no preference.
Take a few minutes,

rest for a spell
as you give a unit of blood
on an inviting donation bed
at the local blood drive,
just waiting for you and me.
I am ready.
I hope you are too.

The On and Off Switch

I am a spigot,
turned on and off
like a light switch

as the phlebotomist pokes a vein.
The blood begins flowing
finding a temporary home in a bag.

Fresh blood,
like pouring a glass of wine into a glass,
then the spigot is turned off,

and the red liquid to be given to another,
to one in great need,
quenching the body's thirst back to health.

Off to the Races

He got onto the donation bed,
the official starting line,
wanting to race his co-worker
in the next lane to see which
one would cross the finishing line first
by filling the bag with a unit of blood.
Forget the track shoes, instead get ready
to squeeze a ball every five seconds,
as the blood flowed from the vein,
through the tube, into the bag.

Off he went, racing on his own,
after his offer was declined,
setting his own personal best with a time
of three minutes and fifty-five seconds,
though his co-worker wasn't far behind
for one who didn't want to race.
Whether a slow poke, a speedster,
or somewhere in between,
everyone was a winner as they
crossed the finish line.

The Blood Drive Comedian

I asked him to read the reading material
since he hadn't earlier that day prior to coming in.
There were fourteen pages in the packet,
none of the words were in fine print, but still,
he said he should have brought along his lawyer,
and I told him he could call one if he wished.

He made it through that phase of the process,
and then the phlebotomist asked if he wanted
something to drink, some water or juice,
replying he would take a beer,
but we were all out, not having any in the first place,
finally settling for a water.

When he got on the table to donate a unit of blood,
he asked if he would live a normal life after giving,
but being a clown, with red nose, long floppy shoes,
he walked away unscathed, and as for a normal life,
I did not know what he considered that to be,
not having lived the clown life myself.

www.ingramcontent.com/pod-product-compliance
Ingram Content Group UK Ltd.
Pitfield, Milton Keynes, MK11 3LW, UK
UKHW041315190726
13845UKWH00025B/284

9 788182 538405